CONSTRUCT IT
Building an Argument

Gillian Gosman

PowerKiDS
press
New York

Published in 2015 by The Rosen Publishing Group, Inc.
29 East 21st Street, New York, NY 10010

First Edition

Editor: Caitie McAneney
Book Design: Mickey Harmon

Photo Credits: Cover (image), p. 22 Hurst Photo/Shutterstock.com; cover (background) Attitude/Shutterstock.com; pp. 3–10, 12–14, 16–32 (dot backgrounds) vlastas/Shutterstock.com; p. 5 (billboard) Rafal Olechowski/Shutterstock.com; p. 5 (rollercoaster) Rodolpho Arpia/Shutterstock.com; p. 5 (pterodactyls) Valentyna Chukhlyebova/Shutterstock.com; p. 5 (T. rex) leonello calvetti/Shutterstock.com; p. 5 (sky) DeiMosz/Shutterstock.com; p. 6 Pressmaster/Shutterstock.com; p. 7 lightwavemedia/Shutterstock.com; p. 8 lxMaster/Shutterstock.com; p. 9 holbox/Shutterstock.com; pp. 11, 18 Monkey Business Images/Shutterstock.com; p. 13 Susan Law Cain/Shutterstock.com; p. 15 iofoto/Shutterstock.com; p. 16 Tyler Olsen/Shutterstock.com; p. 17 Protasov AN/Shutterstock.com; p. 19 Blend Images/Shutterstock.com; p. 21 Ollyy/Shutterstock.com; p. 23 Dmytro Vietrov/Shutterstock.com; p. 25 Monashee Frantz/OJO Images/Getty Images; p. 27 Cultura RM/Gary John Norman/Getty Images; p. 28 B Calkins/Shutterstock.com; p. 29 Tetra Images/Brand X Pictures/Getty Images; p. 30 Gary John Norman/Iconica/Getty Images.

Library of Congress Cataloging-in-Publication Data

Gosman, Gillian.
Construct it: building an argument / by Gillian Gosman.
p. cm. — (Core skills)
Includes index.
ISBN 978-1-4777-7382-6 (pbk.)
ISBN 978-1-4777-7383-3 (6-pack)
ISBN 978-1-4777-7381-9 (library binding)
1. Persuasion (Rhetoric) — Juvenile literature. 2. English language — Rhetoric — Juvenile literature. I. Gosman, Gillian. II. Title.
PE1431.G67 2015
808—d23

Manufactured in the United States of America

CPSIA Compliance Information: Batch #CW15PK: For Further Information contact Rosen Publishing, New York, New York at 1-800-237-9932

CONTENTS

WHAT IS AN ARGUMENT?

Persuasive writing is all around us. You'll find it in every form of printed material—magazines, newspapers, fliers, billboards, and books. To persuade is to sway someone to act or think a certain way. Some real-life examples include persuading people to vote for you in the class election or to believe what you think is true about an issue, such as school uniforms.

At the heart of all persuasive writing is the argument. The argument is a position or opinion about a particular issue. The argument is sometimes called the claim. In this book, we'll learn how to identify your claim, gather **evidence**, and present claims clearly. In successful persuasive writing, the author states an argument, gives reasons to back it up, and often addresses the opposing view.

FAST COASTERS, THE BEST FOOD, AND THE MOST DINOSAURS IN ONE PLACE!

Advertisements often use persuasive writing to get people to buy a certain product. You can find advertisements on billboards, such as this one.

5

PREPARED TO PERSUADE

At some point, you'll be asked by a teacher to present an argument in a piece of persuasive writing. The assignment might be to write a book review, **debate** a political issue, or defend a **hypothesis** in science class. In each case, you'll need to define the issue and identify your position, or point of view. Then, you'll need to gather and present evidence, and be prepared to address other points of view.

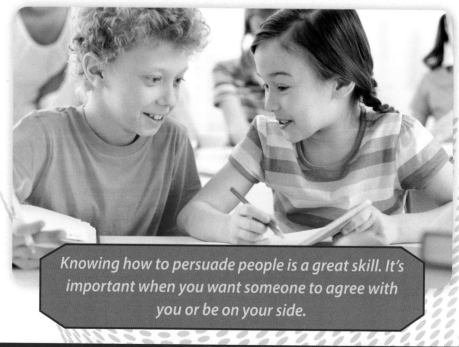

Knowing how to persuade people is a great skill. It's important when you want someone to agree with you or be on your side.

Adults have to use persuasive writing often, and someday you will, too. Someday, you'll write a cover letter to apply for a job. Cover letters try to persuade an employer to hire you. You might also use persuasive writing to express your opinion about a local or national issue in a newspaper or online.

KEEP IT FOCUSED

The first step in persuading an **audience** is choosing a topic and your argument. It's important to make sure your argument is focused on a specific topic. For example, if you want to write about animal rights, you could focus on one particular part of that issue. A more focused topic could be outlawing the use of chinchilla fur for clothing. Since this topic is narrow, it will be easier to organize your thoughts and evidence.

QUICK TIP

Take a close look at the language you use in your argument. Is every sentence clear and focused? A strong argument uses words that have great meaning, such as "beneficial" or "profitable." It doesn't simply say that something is "good" or "bad."

Now, consider your position on the topic. Are you in favor of outlawing the chinchilla fur trade? Are you against it? Why do you feel that way? What kinds of laws and rights do you want to consider? Is your focus your state, the nation, or the whole world?

Common Kinds of Claims

▷ *Claims of fact: Argue whether something is or is not an agreed fact.*

▷ *Claims of value: Argue the importance of something.*

▷ *Claims of solution: Argue a possible solution to a problem.*

▷ *Claims of cause and effect: Argue a cause-and-effect relationship between events.*

STRUCTURE

A persuasive, or argumentative, essay usually sticks to a basic format. It begins with an introduction that lays out the issue and presents your thesis statement. A thesis statement defines your point of view on the issue. An example of a thesis statement is "Our school should increase the **budget** for music programs." This sentence presents the author's position on the school's budget.

The body paragraphs are next. Each body paragraph should present a reason that supports your thesis statement. Each reason should be supported by evidence. Then, you can spend at least one paragraph talking about the opposing view and why you believe it's wrong, using strong evidence. End your essay with a conclusion of your thoughts on the topic.

QUICK TIP

Your teacher may have a particular format for your assignment depending on the class subject, the content, and your audience. A paper written for a science class using laboratory evidence might be structured differently than a paper written for history class using historical **research**. Be sure to follow your teacher's guidelines.

Make sure you use evidence from reliable sources. Reliable sources include original accounts from a time period, articles written by experts, and websites from governments and established organizations. We'll talk more about reliable sources in the following chapters.

EXPLORE THE EVIDENCE

After creating an effective thesis statement, the most important part of an argumentative essay is the evidence. You want to make sure you find evidence from reliable sources so you know it's true and useful to your argument.

There are two kinds of research you can use for evidence: firsthand and secondhand. Firsthand research is research you perform yourself. This may be in the form of interviews, laboratory experiments, exploration, or personal experience. Secondhand research is research performed by others. You might find it in books, articles, movies, and sound recordings, and on reliable websites.

QUICK TIP

Facts in the form of numbers are called statistics. Statistics are great for supporting an argument about science, politics, issues in society, and history. For example, in an argumentative essay about saving coral reefs, you may use the statistic that 58 percent of coral reefs are at risk from human development.

Both firsthand and secondhand research
can be appropriate for supporting your argument.
Different sources are useful at different times.
For example, you may need to use firsthand research
to present information you found through a
laboratory experiment.

When doing secondhand research, you can use primary
sources or secondary sources. Primary sources are original
documents or objects from a certain time period, such as a
diary. Secondary sources *interpret* primary sources, such as
a biography written about a person from the time period.

CITE YOUR SOURCES

Whether you use primary or secondary sources, you need to give credit to their creators. That's called citing a source. There are two types of citations you should use.

In the body of your essay, you should include a parenthetical citation anywhere there is a fact or quote from somebody else's work. A parenthetical citation is a note identifying the author's last name and the page number where the information or quotation appears. You put it in parentheses following the text you borrowed. For example, you might write "(Darwin 24)" when quoting a line from a book by Charles Darwin.

The second step in citing a source is creating a bibliography, which appears after the last page of your essay. A bibliography is an alphabetical list of every source cited in your essay.

> There are several common ways to write bibliography entries. The most popular are the Chicago Manual of Style format (often called "Chicago Style") and the Modern Languages Association format (MLA).

QUICK TIP

Failure to correctly cite any of the information or ideas in your essay can be considered plagiarism. "Plagiarism" means copying words and ideas from another source without giving credit.

15

EVIDENCE AT THE LIBRARY

Ready to find evidence? The library is the spot! Most libraries have online catalogs, which are computer programs or websites that tell you which books a library has and which books they can get from other libraries. You can access the library's online catalog from home or at the library. Search the catalog for words related to your topic.

Once you've found a book that interests you, skim the table of contents to see what it covers. If the book looks promising, you might also check its bibliography and see if your library has any of the books the author used in their research. You might also check the bookshelf where the book is kept, where you will often find other books on the same topic. Also, you can ask your librarian. They're experts in finding the right book!

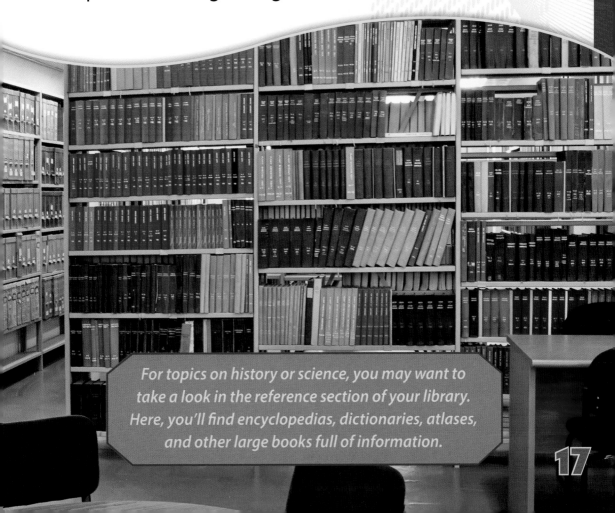

For topics on history or science, you may want to take a look in the reference section of your library. Here, you'll find encyclopedias, dictionaries, atlases, and other large books full of information.

LOOK IT UP ONLINE

Even expert researchers may begin their exploration of a topic with a quick Internet search. Reliable search engines can give you an overview of your topic and **links** to find out more.

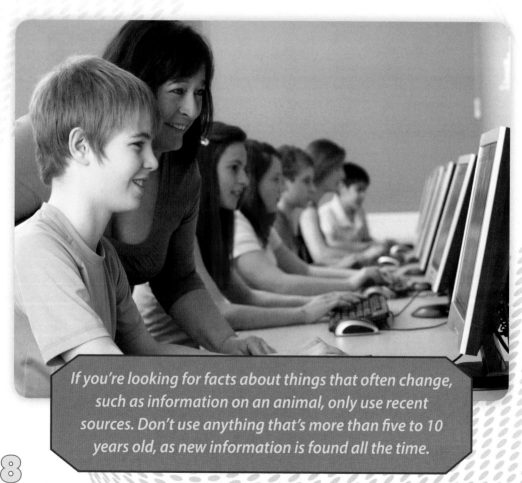

If you're looking for facts about things that often change, such as information on an animal, only use recent sources. Don't use anything that's more than five to 10 years old, as new information is found all the time.

QUICK TIP

If you're doing an online search, it can be helpful to only look at websites that end in .org, .edu, or .gov. Those are usually the endings of website links for organizations, colleges and universities, and government departments.

The major concern with online resources is **reliability**. The Internet allows anyone to create and share all kinds of content, even if it's not correct. Reliable online sources include websites created by colleges and universities, the government, and major news outlets, as well as zoos, museums, and research organizations. Be careful when reading online content created by people not connected with these kinds of organizations. Never rely on information that you read in online **forums**.

If you're wondering about a website's reliability, look for the author or organization. Is it a well-known organization? Is the author an expert?

CRITICAL READING

You've gathered a great collection of resources at the library and online. Now, it's time to be a critical reader. Critical readers question what the author is really saying by studying *how* they say it. They question the author's purpose, reasoning, and reliability. They look for **bias** in any source as suggested by the text's content, tone, and structure. For example, an article about a certain political candidate will likely be biased if someone in the opposing political party wrote it. It may also be biased if someone in the candidate's party wrote it.

As you read, ask yourself the following questions: Is the author providing examples and statistics to support claims? Is the author trying to sway the reader's emotions? For example, are they hoping to get the reader's sympathy?

QUICK TIP

Not everything you read is true! A reliable source will have plenty of statistics and expert reports that can be verified, or proven true. It's good to search many sources to confirm that a fact you found is true and unbiased.

Not sure if a source is reliable?
Ask yourself the following questions:

▷ *Who is the author? Are they known as an expert in the field? Does the author have enough education or professional experience to write about a topic?*

▷ *When was the source created? Look for the most recent source, especially with scientific sources, because there are new discoveries all the time.*

▷ *What is the author's intent? Is the author writing a persuasive essay or article, or a book-length exploration of a topic? Is the author being paid to create the source?*

CRITICAL THINKING

As you work on becoming a critical reader, you must also practice critical thinking. Critical thinking means studying the information presented in a text and then deciding whether or not you accept the author's claims as your own.

To be a strong critical thinker, it's important to stay open-minded about the topic, even after you've written your thesis statement. You have to rely on evidence and realize when your own bias clouds your thinking about a topic. For example, if you're writing a paper on recycling, you should stay true to the evidence you find, even if it goes against what you originally thought. Being a strong critical thinker is a lot of work, and it takes your full attention when you're reading.

You should consider the information in many reliable sources, even if the information goes against your thesis. That will make you a good critical thinker!

WRITING FOR AN AUDIENCE

Are you presenting your argument to your teacher, your class, your whole school, or a youth organization? It's important to understand your audience and write your essay so that it's appropriate. How can you make your audience understand your topic? How can you present evidence clearly?

You may only share your first argumentative essay with your teacher, but you should write with a larger audience in mind. Make sure to explain your topic clearly and show that you have a strong grasp of the material. Assume your reader is less familiar with your topic than you are.

In your argument, make the strongest case possible. Assume your reader is undecided on the issue, and then impress them with the **logic** and depth of your argument.

Will your audience understand the language you use? Use age-appropriate language and avoid difficult words or phrases. Define uncommon terms and explain historical background.

YOUR REBUTTAL

A counterclaim is a view held by others who oppose your argument. In your argumentative essay, you can present a counterclaim and then use evidence to prove why it isn't true. That's called a rebuttal. This is your chance to connect with readers who may not yet be convinced by your argument. It's very important to be polite and logical when you're presenting a counterclaim and proving its shortcomings. This will show your audience that you're not being biased.

To find your counterclaim, consider the common arguments made by supporters of an opposing viewpoint. Don't include an opposing claim that's made only by extremists, or people on the edges of a movement or group. That's not a good representation of what the movement or group actually believes.

QUICK TIP

Your rebuttal should recognize the logic and reasonableness of the counterclaim, while clearly explaining why the counterclaim is untrue or not supported by strong evidence.

If you're pro-recycling, you might present this counterclaim: "Some people believe home recycling isn't worth the effort because most waste comes from businesses, not homes." Then, you can refute that counterclaim with statistics and accounts from experts that say home recycling is actually very useful in saving our environment.

PUTTING IT ALL TOGETHER

Even as you research, begin to organize the information you're gathering. You can use tables, charts, or other diagrams to help you organize your findings. You can break down your findings under different headings. Each heading will develop into a certain reason in support of your thesis statement. Each reason will then be developed and defended in a separate body paragraph.

If you're writing a paper, format your paper the way your teacher prefers. If they prefer a heading and title, make sure to add that. Also include page numbers, parenthetical citations, and a bibliography. This will make it easy to read your paper and refer to the sources you used.

Ask your teacher which format they prefer for citations. Some papers, especially scientific papers, cite their sources using footnotes, or notes at the bottom of a page.

THE PRESENTATION

Your teacher may ask you to present your argument in an oral, or spoken, presentation. They may allow you to use digital presentation tools, such as a slide show or a short film. Choose your visual aids wisely. Make sure any images or digital tools you present are meaningful to your argument and easy to see.

Speak slowly, clearly, and with confidence during your presentation. Know your argument and evidence well so you're prepared to answer questions and rebut counterclaims from your audience.

Do you like building and presenting arguments? You may consider joining your school's debate team, if there is one. You may consider being a lawyer or politician someday. Presenting arguments in a clear, logical, and respectful way is a strong skill that you can use every day!

GLOSSARY

audience (AW-dee-uhns) A group of people who see, hear, or read something.

bias (BY-uhs) A personal preference for or dislike of something or someone.

budget (BUH-juht) A plan to spend a certain amount of money in a period of time.

debate (dih-BAYT) To argue.

evidence (EH-vuh-duhns) Facts that prove something.

forum (FOHR-uhm) An online message board where people share their opinions on a topic.

hypothesis (hy-PAH-thuh-suhs) Something that is suggested to be true for the purpose of an experiment or argument.

interpret (ihn-TUHR-pruht) To explain the meaning of something.

link (LINK) A string of symbols that connects to a certain website.

logic (LAH-jihk) Clear thoughts based on facts.

reliability (rih-ly-uh-BIH-luh-tee) The extent to which a person or source can be trusted.

research (REE-suhrch) The gathering of facts about a subject.

INDEX

WEBSITES

Due to the changing nature of Internet links, PowerKids Press has developed an online list of websites related to the subject of this book. This site is updated regularly. Please use this link to access the list: www.powerkidslinks.com/cosk/cons